CROCODILE ENCOUNTERS!

And More True Stories of Adventures With Animals

Published by the National Geographic Society
John M. Fahey, Jr., *Chairman of the Board and Chief Executive Officer*
Timothy T. Kelly, *President*
Declan Moore, *Executive Vice President; President, Publishing and Digital Media*
Melina Gerosa Bellows, *Executive Vice President; Chief Creative Officer, Books, Kids, and Family*

Prepared by the Book Division
Hector Sierra, *Senior Vice President and General Manager*
Nancy Laties Feresten, *Senior Vice President, Editor in Chief, Children's Books*
Jonathan Halling, *Design Director, Books and Children's Publishing*
Jay Sumner, *Director of Photography, Children's Publishing*
Jennifer Emmett, *Editorial Director, Children's Books*
Eva Absher-Schantz, *Managing Art Director, Children's Books*
Carl Mehler, *Director of Maps*
R. Gary Colbert, *Production Director*
Jennifer A. Thornton, *Director of Managing Editorial*

Staff for This Book
Becky Baines, Laura F. Marsh, *Project Editors*
Lori Epstein, *Illustrations Editor*
Eva Absher-Schantz, *Art Director*
YAY! Design, *Designer*
Grace Hill, *Associate Managing Editor*
Joan Gossett, *Production Editor*
Lewis R. Bassford, *Production Manager*
Susan Borke, *Legal and Business Affairs*
Kate Olesin, *Assistant Editor*
Kathryn Robbins, *Design Production Assistant*
Hillary Moloney, *Illustrations Assistant*

Manufacturing and Quality Management
Phillip L. Schlosser, *Senior Vice President*
Chris Brown, *Vice President, NG Book Manufacturing*
George Bounelis, *Vice President, Production Services*
Nicole Elliott, *Manager*
Rachel Faulise, *Manager*
Robert L. Barr, *Manager*

Trade paperback ISBN: 978-1-4263-1028-7
Reinforced library edition ISBN:
978-1-4263-1029-4

Printed in China
12/RRDS/1

Table of CONTENTS

That's me, zoologist Brady Barr, dressed in a special crocodile suit. My disguise let me get close to the crocs and collect information.

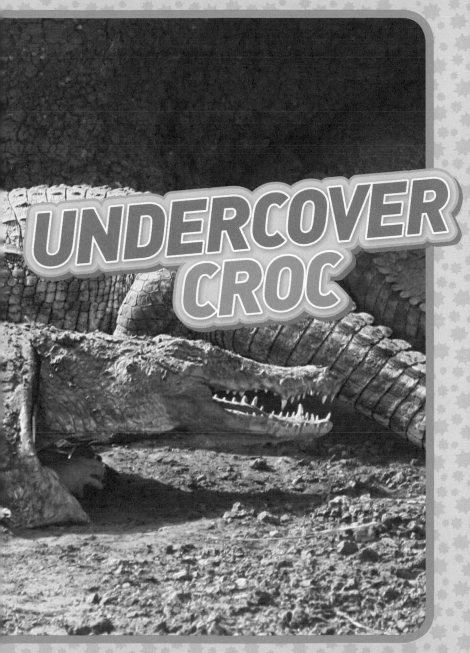

UNDERCOVER CROC

My team and I are ready for our dangerous mission in Tanzania.

Chapter 1

Croc DISGUISE

Hi, my name is Brady Barr, and I'm a zoologist. That means I study animals. I've studied all kinds of animals in about 70 countries on Earth. But of all the animals I've worked with, crocodiles are my favorite.

There are 23 different types, or species, of crocodilians (sounds like krah-koh-DIL-ee-uhns). I've had the chance to see them all in the wild. I've been up close to the wide-snouted alligators and caimans (sounds like KAY-mens). I've been nose-to-nose with the narrow-jawed crocodiles. And I've even studied the weird and wonderful gharial (sounds like GAR-ree-uhl).

Sometimes I have to catch wild crocodiles for my work. For some studies, my team and I need to weigh and measure crocs. For other studies, we need to attach high-tech devices to the crocs. These devices help us keep track of the crocs, or they record information about changes in the areas where the crocs live.

The number of people on Earth is growing every year. More humans on the planet means people need more space. People are moving into areas that were once the wild homes, or habitats, of crocs. With their habitats shrinking, many species of crocodilians are dying out. When a species is dying out, we say it is an endangered species.

The more we know about endangered species and what they need, the better we can help them. But catching wild crocs is a dangerous job—for me and for the crocs!

To catch a croc, I usually have to snare it with a rope. Then I wrestle it until it is very tired. I jump onto its back and tie its jaws shut so it can't bite. Then I tie its legs. That's a lot easier said than done!

Even a tired crocodile is very strong. Catching one can turn dangerous quickly. Crocodiles are not used to having people jump on their backs. It is strange for them.

Endangered Crocs

About one-third of all croc species are endangered. In fact, many are among the most endangered animals on the planet. The Philippine crocodile used to live in lakes and rivers throughout the Philippines (sounds like FILL-ih-peens). Today it is only found in a few areas. As the number of humans has grown, more and more of its wild habitat has been turned into farmland.

Loss of habitat has driven the Philippine crocodile almost to extinction. Once a species is extinct, it's gone forever.

That's why I am always looking for better ways to handle the crocs and get the information we need.

We know that crocodiles are calmer around other crocs than around humans. If only another croc could find out what we need to know. Then it wouldn't be so hard on the animal we want to study.

Well, on a trip to Tanzania (sounds like Tan-zan-EE-uh), I got to find out what it feels like to be a croc.

It all started when I was giving a talk to a group of children at their school. I was telling them about my work with crocodiles. One small boy raised his hand.

"Dr. Brady," he asked, "why don't you dress up as a croc and join their club?"

At the time, I thought that was pretty

funny. I laughed and went on with my talk. But I couldn't shake the idea from my mind. *Could it actually work?* I wondered. There was one way to find out!

I asked the people at National Geographic if they could build me a life-like crocodile suit. Luckily, they were up for the job!

Artists made the head from a mold of a real crocodile head. That made it look exactly like the real thing! It was made of a material called polystyrene (sounds like pahl-ee-STYE-reen). It is very lightweight, but strong.

Next, the engineers built the body. This part was important. It needed to protect my body if an angry croc decided to bite!

They made a set of metal ribs. These formed a strong cage around me. Then the cage was covered by a shield made of Kevlar. The same stuff is used to make bulletproof vests. That would make it hard for even a croc bite to break through!

Finally, the artists made a rubber cape that looked just like crocodile skin. This would cover the body and make it look like a real croc.

At last, my croc suit was ready. And boy, did it look real! My plan was to get close enough to a group of wild crocs to put high-tech devices on their backs. If my test was going to work, I would have to make the crocs believe I was one of them.

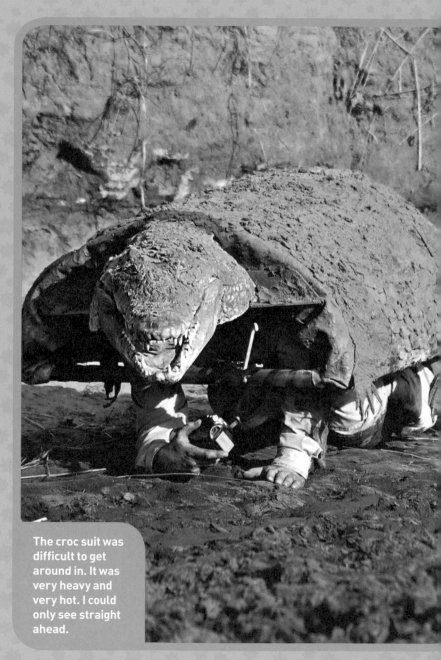

The croc suit was difficult to get around in. It was very heavy and very hot. I could only see straight ahead.

Chapter 2

Dangerous MISSION

A few months later, I was ready to join a bunch of big, wild crocs in Tanzania. I chose Tanzania because it has a lot of crocs. It also has extreme wet and dry seasons.

In the wet season, the crocs spread out over the wetlands. That makes them hard to find.

But in the dry season, the rivers begin to dry up. This creates many separate pools. The crocs are forced to share these shrinking pools. This makes it much easier to find large groups of crocs.

When I got to Tanzania, a fellow scientist was there to help me. His name is Dr. Hannes Botha. He is a croc expert from South Africa.

Hannes and I have worked together many times over the years. We have captured huge crocs together. It is always comforting to work with a friend, someone you know and trust. This is especially true when capturing dangerous animals.

A group of people would help with our experiment. Hannes and I were the two scientists in the group. We also had a wildlife ranger. He would help keep us safe from lions, leopards, and other animals that might want to eat us. And we had two brave National Geographic camera people.

This seemed like a small crew—at least to go after one of the largest predators on the planet: giant Nile crocodiles!

I squeezed my body into the tight suit. The thermometer inside read 120 degrees. *I might cook in this suit if I'm inside too long!* I thought.

My heart beat faster as I thought of the dangerous crocs a short distance away. There was also a herd of hippos I would have to crawl through to get to the crocs!

Everyone knows crocs are dangerous. What many people don't know is that the hippo is Africa's most dangerous animal.

Hippos aren't meat eaters, but they are

very territorial. You don't want to make them feel threatened if you are on their turf. And if a croc gets too close to a hippo's baby, watch out! The hippo can bite the croc in half. I would have to stay away from the hippo babies.

Once inside the suit, I felt really sick and really scared. The suit weighed more than 80 pounds. It was very heavy, and I felt very cramped. But the worst part was the smell. We had smeared hippo poop all over it. It was important to cover up my human smell.

Soon it was time to go. My crew stepped back quietly. They hid themselves as well as they could. I started to crawl toward the crocs.

I could only see straight ahead because of my suit. I could not see to the sides or in back of me. But I could talk to my crew using my walkie-talkie. They would warn me if any angry crocs or hippos were moving toward me. It was great to have radio contact with my buddies. I needed to ask them for directions and help. It was good to hear their voices. Then I didn't feel so alone. It was very scary to be crawling around with danger on all sides.

To get to the crocs, I needed to crawl through the herd of hippos. Hippos can weigh three tons. That's 6,000 pounds. They can run like the wind. And they don't welcome intruders.

The Scoop
on Hippo Poop

Hippos don't drop their poop like most animals. When a hippo has to go, its tail starts swishing back and forth very fast. Then the hippo lets loose with an explosive shower of poop. It flies through the air and covers everything. It's called a dung shower.

Hippos do this to mark their territory. One whiff of that dung and you'd want to stay away, too! The hippo dung on my croc suit was so strong, the crocs and hippos couldn't smell my human smell. It was a good—but smelly—disguise.

I knew the hippos were aware I was there. They were giving me the stare-down. Then I heard them wheeze-honking.

Wheeze-honking is a super-loud sound. It's something like a deep laugh. And it's followed by a *hurumph-hurumph-hurumph!* Believe me, it is frightening to hear nervous hippos wheeze-honking all around you.

Luckily, the hippos didn't bother me. I kept crawling through the herd. As I got near the crocs, my heart was pounding. My mouth was dry, and my body was shaking.

Yet, my senses were razor sharp—sharper than they had ever been before. I held my breath and inched closer. I had no idea what would happen next.

Humans only have two sets of teeth, but crocs lose teeth and grow new ones throughout their lifetime.

Then I saw it. Right in front of me! I came eye-to-eye with a croc. And its eyes were glued on me!

I had never seen a crocodile from a croc's-eye view before. Boy, did it look big!

The animal was beautiful—and scary! I was close enough to reach out and touch it. The croc kept staring at me.

Then, much to my relief, the big croc calmly closed its eyes. Clearly, it was not going to let me disturb its nap. This was a sign that the animal was okay with me being there.

I was within three feet of a wild croc. And it seemed to be accepting me as another croc. Amazing! The heat, the heavy suit, the sickening smell of the hippo poop—all those bad things seemed to just disappear. I was a crocodile among crocodiles! No one had ever done this before. I was totally caught up in the excitement of the moment.

Then, suddenly, my attention was jolted back to the dangers around me. One of my camera people radioed me. A large croc was moving toward me from behind.

Cool, Creative Lab

Let me take you behind the scenes to the National Geographic Lab!

The lab is a workshop where engineers and artists hang out. It's in the basement of the National Geographic building in Washington, D.C. It is an awesome and amazing place!

At any time, you might find them building mini-submarines. They also build remote-controlled helicopter cameras, and they construct seal decoys for sharks to attack. They can put together just about anything you could dream up!

I froze. My heart raced once again. I held my breath, waiting for an attack. Would my croc suit protect me from the bite of a half-ton giant?

Seconds seemed like hours, as I waited for the croc. I could hear its heavy feet slogging through the mud toward me. It moved closer. I could hear it breathing.

Did You Know?

Data-loggers are electronic devices, about the size of a quarter. They can be programmed to collect and store temperature readings over time.

But then . . . nothing happened. The attack I feared never came. Instead, the croc rubbed up beside me and lay down. It was accepting me as one of the crocs! I could hardly believe it.

Still, anything could happen. Another croc could attack me at any minute. I wanted to make history on this day—not become history!

It was time for action. I reached out to the croc in front of me. I glued a small data-logger to the croc's back. The data-logger was set up to sense temperature changes in the croc's area. It would record the temperature every five minutes.

Once I was sure the device was working, I pulled my arm in. Then I got out of there. I crawled away from the crocs as quickly as I could.

My undercover experiment had worked. On this day, I had become a crocodile. Just as the boy at the school had suggested, I had joined the crocodile club!

I am practicing with my remote-controlled toy car. Can I catch a croc with it?

Catching crocs is never easy—or clean.

Chapter 1

A PLAN TO Catch a Croc

Crocodiles are very, very hard to catch. First, you have to find them, and that's tougher than it sounds. The texture and color of their skin blends in with their surroundings. And crocs know how to get around without being seen or heard.

Even if you're lucky enough to find a croc, it's still not easy to catch one. Why? Because crocs have keen senses. They have good eyesight, great hearing, and a super sense of smell. They can sense the slightest change in anything around them. That makes it almost impossible to get close to them.

Usually, the best time to find and catch crocs is at night. In the dark, their eyes give them away. Croc eyes look like glowing red coals when you shine a spotlight at them. You can see them from really far away, too—even as far away as the length of a few football fields.

Croc eyes have a special lining. When light hits the lining, it bounces back.

Did You Know?

Like cats' eyes, crocs' eyes have slit-like pupils. That kind of pupil gives crocs a lot of control over how much light enters their eyes.

That's called eyeshine. It's the same thing you see when you use a camera flash to take a picture of your pet dog or cat. Their eyes will sometimes have a spooky yellow glow in the picture.

This special lining in crocs' eyes helps them see in dim light. Other animals that are active at night have it, too.

When I'm trying to catch crocs at night, I shine my powerful light across the water. I am looking for eyeshines. Once I see one, I slowly inch toward the croc.

I keep the spotlight on its eyes the whole time. The croc can't see me coming because of the bright light shining in its eyes. I can sneak in close enough to get a rope around its neck. This is not as easy as it sounds.

Night Vision

Animals that are active at night must be able to see in the dark. They have a special lining at the back of their eyes called the tapetum lucidum (sounds like tuh-pee-tum loo-sid-um). The tapetum lucidum is like a mirror. It bounces light back toward the cornea (COR-nee-ah), which is the outer lens of the eye. This helps crocs see better in low light.

For every ten crocs I get close to, I'm lucky to catch just one. Catching crocs is hard, so I am always looking for new ways to get near them.

I get many of my best ideas from kids. Once again, I was speaking to a group of elementary school kids. As I often do, I asked them for their ideas on ways to catch crocs, especially during the day. The kids made drawings to explain their ideas.

My favorite idea of all was to use a remote-controlled (R/C) toy car. I had told the kids that every morning, crocodiles crawl out of the water and lie in the sun. We call this basking. The crocs do this to get warm.

Humans are mammals, and mammals are warm-blooded. This means that their body temperature stays about the same, no matter where they are. Crocodiles are reptiles, and they are cold-blooded. They need to lie in the sun to warm up. They need to crawl into the shade or water to cool down. That is how they control their body temperature.

The kids figured that a good time to catch crocs is when they are basking on the beach. Remember, though, crocs are almost impossible to get close to—basking or not. But the kids had that all figured out! I would not try to get near the crocs myself. I would drive an R/C car to them.

The plan was simple. I would attach a pole to the front of the car. I'd hang a rope with a loop from the pole. The end of the rope would be tied to a plastic milk jug. That would work as a float.

Next I would drive the car over to a basking croc. When the car was close enough, I would try to slip the rope over the croc's head. Once the rope was on, I was supposed to scare the croc. The croc would jump into the water. It would pull the rope and floating milk jug behind it as it swam away.

Then I would get into my boat and follow the float. When I got close, I could grab the float. I'd use the rope to pull the croc up. And then I would have caught it! This idea sounded awesome! It was genius! And I would get to play with a cool toy.

Nile crocodiles have big mouths and lots of teeth. They are fierce predators but rarely attack people.

Chapter 2

The Great CHASE

I was ready to get to work. I got myself an R/C car and attached a pole and rope to the front of it.

I practiced by trying to catch my dog, Margie. I soon found out that Margie was a lot quicker than a croc! In fact, Margie learned that it was more fun to chase my R/C car than to have it chase her.

After a few weeks, I decided I was ready to try catching a croc.

Margie was happy, too. She had grown tired of her game.

I packed up my R/C car and set off for South Africa. I headed straight to the Olifants (sounds like OLE-i-fonts) River. The Olifants has loads of crocs and lots of nice basking sites. I would be meeting up with my old buddy and fellow croc scientist, Dr. Hannes Botha.

Hannes has studied the crocs of the Olifants for many years. He probably knows more about them than does anyone else on the planet. Also, the river is right in his backyard. So, who better to help me with this new experiment?

I was so sure that this idea was going to work, I decided to attach a small video camera to the R/C car. I would film it all.

A River of Crocs

The Olifants River is in South Africa. Olifants means "elephant" in the local language. It may be called the Elephant River, but man, it sure has a lot of Nile crocs!

The river flows north through Kruger National Park, South Africa's largest national park. There it winds its way through a beautiful canyon called Olifants Gorge. Olifants Gorge has been called the Grand Canyon of Kruger National Park. It looks like the Grand Canyon in the United States, only smaller.

I wanted to show the kids back home how their great idea worked.

Everything was in order. Bright and early the next morning, the crocs started crawling out of the water. They settled on the sunny beach to warm themselves. I had my R/C car all charged up and ready. The video camera, rope, and milk jug were all attached. It was time to put this idea to the test. It was GO time!

From a long distance away, I gently placed my car on the beach. I started driving it toward the crocs. As the car got closer, the crocs began to notice it. I think they were uneasy about this strange little thing coming toward them.

One by one, the crocs slid into the water. I was very disappointed. The closer the car got, the more crocs went into the water. I was beginning to doubt this idea would work. But I kept the car going.

By the time the car reached the basking area, all the crocs were back in the water. I was very sad that the R/C car had scared them all away. I started driving the car back to me.

Suddenly . . . *BOOM!!! SPLASH!!!* In an instant, a huge croc exploded out of the water. Yikes! This big croc was coming after my car. It wanted to eat it!

The croc snapped its jaws and raced after my R/C car. I drove like crazy to get the car away. I tried to scream, but no sound came out.

This wasn't what we'd planned! I was supposed to drive slowly toward the croc to catch it. Now I was driving full speed away from it. I hoped the croc wouldn't catch my car and eat it!

I could not shake the croc. I would go right. The croc would go right. I went left. The croc turned left. It stayed right on my tail. For a while, everything was just a blur of snapping jaws and hurried fingers working the R/C controls. My hands began shaking. This croc was good, and my driving was getting worse and worse.

The huge croc was getting dangerously close. Finally, I turned right when I should have turned left. *CHOMP!*

It had the car. I heard a sickening *CRUNCH*. The big old croc bit down with its strong jaws. I stood on that sandy beach with my mouth open. I couldn't believe it. The croc calmly crawled back into the water. It had my car and expensive camera in its mouth.

It floated on the surface for a second. Then it threw its big head back. In one quick motion, it swallowed my car and the camera! The croc sank into the water and disappeared. My equipment was gone, and so was the croc.

Minutes later, I was still standing there. I held the R/C controller in my shaking hands. All I could do was stare at the ripples on the water.

This is my camera, covered in mud and croc spit.

Chapter 3

Lost and FOUND

was in big trouble. Not only had I lost my new R/C car. I had also lost an expensive camera that didn't belong to me. What would I tell my boss? I was worried.

It was a long flight home. I finally returned to National Geographic headquarters in Washington, D.C. I had to break the bad news.

I told my boss about the kids'

great idea and the R/C car. And I told him about how it had all gone wrong. I was really sorry about what had happened.

Surprisingly, my boss wasn't too mad. He said I didn't have to pay for the camera. But he hoped I had learned a lesson.

And this is where I thought the story was over. But it wasn't.

Months later, I got a phone call from my friend Hannes. He said, "Brady, you're not going to believe this. I found your R/C car."

I couldn't believe it! What luck!

Crocodiles often swallow things they can't digest. They swallow hard things that look good to them—things like rocks, sticks, and even R/C cars with cameras.

These hard things are called gastroliths (sounds like GAS-tro-liths). The word means "stomach stones." Scientists are not sure exactly why crocs swallow gastroliths. It's a mystery.

Crocs keep gastroliths in their stomachs for a long time. Sometimes they keep them there for weeks or even months. But, eventually, the crocs throw them up.

If you're lucky, you can sometimes find piles of thrown-up gastroliths on basking beaches. That is where Hannes found my camera.

I asked him to mail the camera to me. About a week later, I got the package. I tore it open, and there was my camera!

Big Gulp

Crocs are not the only animals that swallow gastroliths. So do birds like chickens and ostriches. Seals and sea lions do, too.

Scientists are trying to find out what happens inside a croc when it swallows a gastrolith. Some scientists say that the gastrolith helps a croc grind up its food. That is what happens in a chicken's gizzard. Others think that the weight of the gastrolith is important. Swallowing it may allow a croc to float at just the right depth in the water.

Boy, did it smell bad. *Whoooweee!* It was covered in dried croc vomit, and it had bite marks all over it.

But it was still in one piece. As I was checking the camera for damage, I pushed the "eject" button. Out popped the videotape! I couldn't believe it! I knew right away what I had to do: Go see the kids!

I went straight to the elementary school. I didn't show them a video of how our experiment had failed. I did show them how their idea had led to this amazing video. They got to see what the inside of a croc's stomach looks like! And that was good enough for them.

Can you find the hidden croc in its den? Its eye is the only thing not covered in mud!

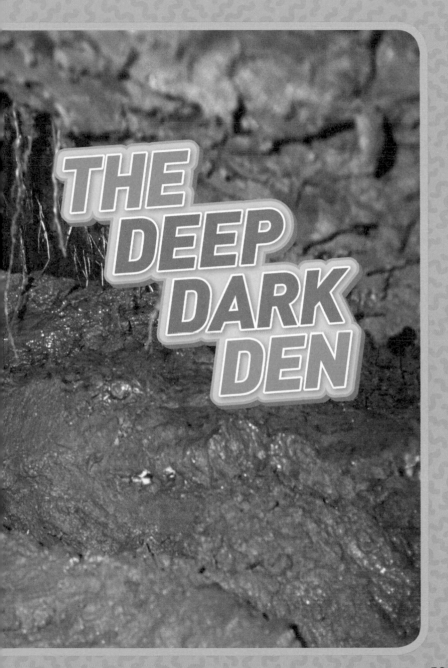

THE DEEP DARK DEN

The American crocodile is an endangered species in nearly all areas of North, Central, and South America.

Chapter 1

DRAINING the Lake

Over the years, people have moved farther and farther into croc habitats. When humans and crocs live close together, they don't always get along. A croc expert is often called in to help when there's trouble.

A few years ago, I went to Costa Rica on a special mission. There were crocodiles living in a lake too close to town. I needed to catch them and move them to a safer place.

They were American crocodiles. You might wonder, *Why was an "American" croc living in Costa Rica?* Well, it is called an American crocodile because it is found in parts of North America, Central America, and South America.

The crocs in this lake were labeled "problem crocs." They were upsetting their human neighbors by attacking dogs, cats, and even cows! No one wants to see their animals hurt. But the crocs were just trying to find food to eat.

There were 13 big crocodiles in the lake. If people weren't careful, they could also be in trouble. Crocodiles can be very dangerous to humans, especially small children. A kid playing along the shore of the lake might not realize there are dangerous crocs in the water. And people out fishing in small boats are also at risk.

The people who lived in the area decided to have the biggest crocodiles moved. They would be taken to a safer place like a national park. There the crocs would find plenty of their natural prey. They would not be forced to eat dogs, cats, and cows.

I was hoping I could help. As soon as I got there, I looked things over.

Crocs are hard to catch when they slip below the surface of the water. Once they dive, they can stay underwater for a long time—sometimes for more than an hour!

This lake was small, so I decided to drain most of the water out of it. With the water level lower, the crocs would be much easier to find and to catch . . . or so I thought!

It took all night for the lake to drain. I used a big pump that sucked water from the lake through a long hose. It carried the water away from the lake with another long hose. It's the same kind of pump people use to drain swimming pools when they need to clean or fix them.

I wasn't exactly going to clean the lake. What I needed was to clean the big crocs out of it!

I let the pump run all night. I woke up a few times and went down to the lake to check on how it was going.

Costa Rican Crocs

Costa Rica is one of my favorite places on the planet. It is a small country—about the size of West Virginia. But it has a ton of different wild animals and habitats!

If you want to see crocs, Costa Rica is awesome! Two species are found in its rivers and swamps: the American crocodile (the same species found in Florida) and the spectacled caiman. The spectacled caiman looks like it's wearing spectacles, or glasses. That's how it got its name.

By early the next morning, the water was really low. It was only about a foot deep in the center. I expected to see 13 crocodiles lying in the mud, waiting to be caught.

Instead, I saw nothing. Zip! Zero crocodiles!

I had seen them with my own eyes just the day before. Where had they gone? Maybe they had walked away, looking for water.

Had they crawled all the way to the river, a mile away? I wanted to find out. I walked along the muddy shore. I looked for croc tracks. Tracks would tell me which way they'd gone.

Big croc footprints are easy to see because, well, they are really, really big!

Crocs have five toes on their front feet. They have four toes on their webbed back feet. A big croc can have a foot that is more than 12 inches long! It's hard to miss those monster tracks.

Crocs also drag their tails when they get up and walk. When you're tracking crocs on land, you'll see a series of footprints. The prints will have a line between them. That line is made by the heavy tail as it drags behind.

I searched every inch of mud, but I couldn't find a single footprint. Did those crazy crocs fly away? It was as if they had simply disappeared!

The entrance to the hole was barely big enough to fit me. Could it fit 13 crocodiles?

Chapter 2

What's in THERE?

"Hey, maybe they're in here!" shouted my friend Juan. Juan Bolanos is a Costa Rican crocodile expert. He has probably captured more crocs in Costa Rica than anyone else. He is a scientist at the National University of Costa Rica. He has taught me all about Costa Rica and its crocs.

Together, Juan and I have caught and moved some really huge crocs over the years. He is my favorite croc-catching buddy in Central America.

Juan was pointing to a small, muddy hole in the ground. He thought that maybe the crocs had all crawled in there.

"No way!" I laughed. "You're telling me 13 crocodiles went down that hole like rabbits?"

Juan laughed, too. "It does seem pretty unlikely," he agreed. "But where else could they be?" We continued our search around the lake, but found no other clues. Only that small hole.

Juan shrugged. "They *must* be down this hole," he said.

I decided to crawl in and have a look. That may have been one of my craziest ideas ever. Holes in the ground in this part of the world can be very unsafe places. Many types of dangerous snakes can be found in such holes. I knew I didn't want to run into a deadly snake!

The opening of the hole was barely large enough for me. I got down on all fours and poked my head in.

"Whoa!" I gasped. It was dark and muddy and scary inside.

I grabbed my flashlight so I could peer into the darkness. Then I took a deep breath. It smelled really bad—like rotten fish. I got down on my belly and slithered into the hole. *Hmmm, this could be a croc burrow,* I thought to myself.

Crocs are great diggers, there's no doubt about that. They can dig burrows with their mouths and front feet.

Did You Know?

In dry seasons, crocs estivate (ES-ti-vate) in burrows. That means they go into a kind of hibernation mode, like bears.

If there isn't enough water or food, crocs dig a burrow and stay down there for a long time. That's because burrows are cool and damp. Crocs can survive there when it becomes too hot and dry outside. They can stay underground without eating or drinking for weeks or even months!

They will usually stay underground until the wet season begins. The water level rises again in their river, swamp, or pond. Only then do the crocs come out to find food and water.

Did draining the lake make the crocs think the dry season had suddenly arrived? I didn't know, but I was going to find out.

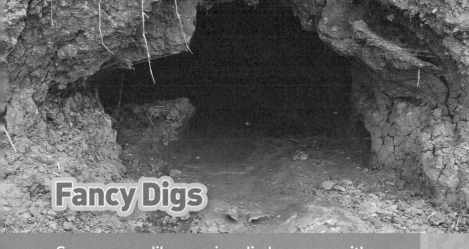

Fancy Digs

Some crocodile species dig burrows with many different tunnels and rooms. Others dig very simple burrows.

The mugger crocodile that lives in India and Sri Lanka (sounds like Sree-LANG-ka) digs a simple burrow. It is shaped like a spoon, with one long, straight tunnel and an oval-shaped room at the end.

The Chinese alligator digs a really fancy burrow with many tunnels and rooms. It sometimes even has an underground pool for drinking and swimming! A house with a swimming pool—it doesn't get any better than that!

I crawled into the hole, armed with only a flashlight.

Chapter 3

BEWARE of Dark Holes!

As I inched down the muddy hole, I looked for any sign of crocs. All I could see were the dark walls of the tunnel.

Nope. No crocs in here, I thought.

Then, as I began backing out, I heard a strange sound coming from deep inside the tunnel. It was a quiet *Sssssss,* like the sound of air being let out of a bike tire.

A croc will sometimes make a hissing sound when it is upset. Snakes hiss like that, too. But I couldn't see any sign of a snake or a crocodile.

I tried to be still and listen more closely. But all I could hear was the pounding of my own heart.

I backed slowly out of the tunnel. "Looks like just a smelly, empty hole," I told Juan.

He didn't seem so sure. Juan wanted to see for himself.

Before I knew it, he had disappeared down the hole. But within seconds he came back out. He was covered in mud from head to toe. There was a blank, wide-eyed look on his face.

"*What?*" I asked.

He just shook his head and backed away from the hole.

At first, I thought maybe Juan had seen a big snake. I knew that a bushmaster could grow to more than ten feet long. That snake is scary and very dangerous. Local people call it the "ox killer" because they say it can bring down a huge ox with its deadly bite. So maybe Juan had seen a bushmaster. I wondered how I could have missed a ten-foot-long snake.

Now I was even more scared than before. Then curiosity got the better of me. I decided I had to look again. I eased back into the hole. Then I slip-slopped through the mud to the place where I'd heard the faint hiss. Where was the darn snake?

I stopped and looked to my left. I looked to my right. I looked up. I peered straight ahead, as far down the tunnel as I could see.

I didn't see a thing. I decided that the snake, or whatever it was, must have crawled away.

Or maybe Juan was seeing things— imagining things that were not there. In the dim light and tight space of the burrow, it's easy to get scared. Your mind can play tricks on you.

I began to back out of the hole, when I heard it again. *Sssssssssss.* This time it was not so quiet!

Crowded With Crocs

Many crocs will sometimes crowd into one burrow at the same time. I have seen burrows filled with dozens and dozens of crocs. I've seen burrows so crowded, there is not one inch of room left inside.

The crocs that can't fit inside will wait patiently outside. It's almost as if it's a hotel, and they're waiting for a room.

For some reason, crocs all seem to get along while inside. They are able to stay calm while they are in a cramped space.

Yikes! I thought. *Maybe Juan had seen a snake after all. A BIG one.*

I turned my headlamp toward the muddy wall. The sound seemed to be coming from there, but I still couldn't see a thing. *Man, I must be hearing things,* I thought.

Again, I tried to hold still and listen. I scanned the wall nervously. That's when something really terrifying happened.

A mud-caked eyelid slowly opened, and a glossy green eye stared straight at me!

The wall was looking back at me! Yikes and double yikes!

What I'd thought was just a muddy wall was really a giant, mud-covered crocodile. And it was just inches from my face! The sound I'd heard was not a snake.

It was this unhappy croc hissing at me.

As I studied the walls of the tunnel more closely, I saw eyes everywhere. I should have backed out of the tunnel that instant.

I was frozen with fear. Then I felt something grab me by my ankles!

Oh no! I thought. *One of the crocs has got me!* It pulled me up out of the hole.

As I blinked in the bright Costa Rican sunlight, I realized the "croc" that had grabbed me was Juan. He had saved me by pulling me out. He, too, had heard the angry croc's hiss. He knew he had to get me out of there fast.

Safely out of the hole, I thanked Juan. And I said to myself, so I wouldn't forget: "Always keep out of dark, scary burrows!"

The big, sturdy wooden box was made especially to move big crocs.

CROC IN A BOX

To capture a large crocodile, you need rope, skill, and a lot of practice.

Chapter 1

Croc on a PLANE?

When crocs cause trouble, it's usually not a big group. Most of the time it's just one. One very big, very smart croc. The largest, most daring crocs are almost always big males. Males can grow to be almost twice the size of females.

This type of croc needs to be captured and moved to a safer place. But if the local people can't do this, they usually have to kill the croc.

A few years ago, the government of Uganda (sounds like Yu-GAN-da) invited me to come and teach their wildlife rangers. They wanted me to show them how to safely capture and relocate problem crocs. This was a big step for them.

Most countries still kill problem crocs. It's really sad. In most cases, it isn't the croc's fault that it's been labeled a "problem." It's the fault of people who are not being careful enough in places where crocs live.

It's a lot easier and cheaper to kill a croc than it is to move it. However, Uganda decided that it is not right to kill these beautiful animals. It decided that saving these crocodiles is worth the cost.

Playing It Safe

Whenever people live close to crocodiles, they must be very careful. They cannot let their kids splash and play along the water's edge. They should not fish while wading in the water. They should not wash clothes in the water or go swimming.

Crocs can easily mistake people for their natural food. When a person is doing something foolish, a croc can hardly be blamed for mistaking that person for something to eat!

So I went to help out the Uganda Wildlife Authority. I started a class for its wildlife rangers. We all began calling it "Croc School"!

Croc School was fantastic. The rangers quickly learned how to catch crocs. At the end of the class, we had a final test. The test was to try to capture a very large, and very naughty, croc.

The croc we were after lived in Lake Victoria, the largest lake in Africa. The croc liked to hang out near a small village. And it had been eating the villagers' cows.

This was a very old and very smart crocodile. Catching it would not be easy.

Luckily, I had my student rangers to help me. We knew if we didn't succeed, the croc would be doomed.

The plan was to catch the croc, and then I would ship it to a zoo in the United States. It would be going to the St. Augustine Alligator Farm and Zoological Park.

This is an amazing zoo—the only one in the world that has every species of croc on display. It would be a great place for our big croc to live in safety. But getting a one-ton, 18-foot crocodile from Africa to the United States is easier said than done.

Before I began, I called several airlines. I asked them if they'd be willing to fly my crocodile to the United States. Every single airline agent laughed at me.

They worried that a big crocodile would break out of its shipping crate. They worried it would crash the airplane!

They said if the reptile got loose, it would thrash around in the belly of the plane. That movement would be enough to throw any aircraft off balance—even a big, stable plane.

I told them it was perfectly safe to ship the crocodile. I explained that another croc expert from the zoo and I would ride with the croc in the plane. I also told them that no croc could ever break out of a sturdy wooden box. That didn't seem to make a difference. The airlines wanted nothing to do with my big croc. Except one.

"Are you absolutely sure the croc will not break out of its container and crash the airplane?" the agent asked.

I explained that no croc could break out of a big, sturdy box. The box we would use was made for moving big crocs. The zoo had used the same type of box to move a giant saltwater croc not long ago. It worked like a charm.

Also, the croc's eyes would be covered while in the box. Any time I'm working with a crocodile, one of the first things I do is cover its eyes. That makes the animal calm down. This is also safer for the people working around the croc. It is less likely to strike out at people if it can't see them.

After many hours, I finally convinced the airline to fly our giant croc, once we had captured it. I was so happy! Now it was time to find this "problem" croc.

My team and I captured this big crocodile. The plan was to move the animal to a safe place.

Chapter 2

Call that CROC IN!

When my crew and I got to the village, I was very nervous! All the villagers had come to the lakeshore to watch us. *I hope we don't disappoint all these people,* I thought to myself. The head wildlife ranger, Peter Ogwang, was with us. There were also three rangers and a small group of villagers. We set off in our dugout canoe.

A dugout is made from a tree trunk that has been hollowed out. The biggest ones hold more than 20 people. Even big dugouts can be pretty tippy in the water.

Going after a huge croc in a tippy dugout canoe may sound a little crazy. Maybe it is. But that really is the best way to get close enough to catch a clever old croc.

Big crocs don't get big by being stupid. They know right away when something is up. If you want to catch them, it is important to blend in.

It would be much safer to go after a croc in a big, fancy powerboat. But the croc would see the boat as something different. It would either hide or be very cautious about getting too close. The dugout canoe—the same kind of boat the locals use for fishing—would be very familiar to the croc.

We hoped we could fool it. But this croc had a lot of practice at outsmarting humans. I knew we were going to need a lot of luck to pull this off.

A couple of hours after dark, we were quietly paddling our canoe.

We hadn't been paddling long when, boy, oh boy, did we get lucky! Within the first hour we spotted our croc.

We were pretty far from shore when I first saw the big, scaly beast. It was swimming out in front of us. It was about as far away as the width of a soccer field.

It was moving from left to right.

Wow, it looked huge! Especially because we were sitting low on the water in our canoe. I have to admit I was a little nervous seeing this giant croc. I was worried about the safety of everyone in the boat.

The croc didn't pay any attention to us, though. It went swimming right past us! We couldn't paddle fast enough to catch it. I had to somehow get the croc to come back toward us. If I didn't do something fast, it was going to be gone.

I quickly decided to use a trick that had worked for me in the past. I was going to try and call that big boy in. That's right—call it in! I started making the sound a baby croc makes when it's in trouble. It's the baby croc's distress call.

"*Whaa, whaaa, whaaaa,*" I called out.

When crocs hear this distress call, they usually come to see what's up. As soon as I let out the first *whaa whaaa*'s, that monster croc changed direction. It turned and headed straight toward us! It looked just like a torpedo coming to sink us.

Everyone in the boat became very nervous. This dangerous croc was bearing down on us. I grabbed my trusty snare pole. It's a long pole with a rope loop on the end. All I had to do was get that rope over the croc's head when it got close. That is, if it didn't eat our boat first! All the men in the boat stopped paddling. They held their breath. Would I catch the croc, or would the croc catch us?

Luckily, the loop slipped right over the curious croc's head. We had it! Everyone on board let out a big sigh of relief.

But getting the rope on the croc turned out to be the easy part. Paddling the croc back to the village behind the canoe was the hard part. We were a long way from shore. And it was like an ocean out on the lake! There were big waves, and our tippy canoe was all over the place. We were trying hard to pull the angry, thrashing croc to shore.

I thought we'd never make it! We had the croc securely roped, but I was still afraid it might get loose. Or worse, it might tip the canoe over. After a whole lot of paddling, we finally got the giant safely to the shore.

Rocket Launcher

Not only does a croc have the strongest jaws on the planet. It has a very powerful tail, too.

A croc uses its tail to swim. It also uses its tail to hurl itself straight out of the water. A crocodile can launch itself like a rocket into the air. It takes a superstrong tail to get 500 to 1,000 pounds of croc clear out of the water.

A croc can grab birds and bats right out of trees. That's a croc's way of grabbing a quick snack!

The box that held the huge crocodile wasn't quite sturdy enough!

Chapter 3

ESCAPE Artist

As we pulled onto the beach back at the village, the people cheered. They could see we had been successful.

Everyone wanted to touch the giant croc. People wanted photos of it. Everyone had a story to tell about his or her own adventures with this wild croc.

Finally, a group of strong men from the village came forward.

They helped us carry the croc from the boat to the sturdy box. That box would be its home for the long flight to the U.S.

We placed the croc gently inside. We blindfolded it and bolted the lid. Now it was safe and secure. That croc wouldn't be getting into any more trouble.

Everyone cheered again. Then a big party began. There was singing, dancing, and lots of good food.

Everyone started chanting "Gwenna! Gwenna! Gwenna!" That means "crocodile" in their local language. I started shouting "Gwenna! Gwenna! Gwenna!" too. We were all very happy.

The party went on until late in the night. Finally, I went to my tent and fell fast asleep.

Rock-a-Bye Baby

When I capture a big croc, I always try to flip it onto its back. Crocs go limp when they are upside down. It's almost as if they are asleep. This is called tonic immobility (TAHN-ick im-mo-BILL-ih-tee). The same thing happens to sharks when they are flipped over.

If you get a croc onto its back, you don't even have to hold it down. It will just lie there as if it cannot move. Sometimes I rub its belly and tell people I am putting it to sleep. But really, it's tonic immobility!

That night, I dreamed about the big old croc. I dreamed about the sturdy wooden box and the long flight home. What fun it would be to arrive in the U.S. with . . .

"Hey! Hey!" The sound of men shouting woke me.

"Wake up! Hurry!" the voices cried.

Outside my tent, I found several men yelling and pointing. It was early in the morning. The sun was barely up. I was still half asleep and very confused.

"What's happened?" I asked.

One of the men grabbed me by the arm. He pulled me toward an excited crowd. They were gathered around the crocodile's crate. Everyone was shouting and talking loudly. As we got closer, the people stopped talking and moved aside.

I couldn't believe my eyes. I rubbed them wearily and looked again. *No*, I thought, *this just isn't possible.* I stood there, stunned.

Right there in front of me was the big, sturdy wooden box. It had a big hole in the side of it. The crocodile had escaped!

I was wrong about the power of a big crocodile. To this day, I still have no idea how that croc broke out of that box!

I took a deep breath and called the airline that had agreed to ship the croc. "You were right," I told the agent. "And I, the crocodile expert, was wrong. I have found at least one big croc that *can* break out of a big, sturdy wooden box."

Next time I catch a big croc, I think I'll use a big, sturdy *metal* box!

THE END

DON'T MISS!

NATIONAL GEOGRAPHIC KIDS CHAPTERS

TIGER IN TROUBLE!

And More True Stories of Amazing Animal Rescues

By Kelly Milner Halls

NATIONAL GEOGRAPHIC

Turn the page for a sneak preview . . .

Nitro's Kansas home was a tiny cage in a junkyard.

Junkyard JUNGLE

Ten-year-old Nitro paced in his cage. It was the evening of February 21, 2009. The sun was setting quickly. Nitro's owner, Jeffrey Harsh, was late with the tiger's dinner.

Hungry big cats get restless, but Nitro couldn't pace far. His chain-link cage was only 20 feet wide and 30 feet long—one-third the size of a school gym. Nitro was eight feet long. He could only take a few steps. Then he had to turn and walk the other way. Back and forth. Back and forth.

He stepped over bones in the dust. They were left over from earlier meals. He brushed against Apache, the other tiger in his cage. His empty belly grumbled. He growled and roared.

Nitro and Apache were not alone. There were three female lions in other cages nearby. All of these big cats were living at the Prairie Cat Animal Refuge near Oakley, Kansas—and they were all hungry.

A man wandered to the main gate. The cats' eyes locked on him. He opened the gate and slowly came inside.

The man passed piles of junk.
He looked into each animal's cage. Nitro
listened, while the other cats studied
the stranger.

Then the man walked toward a lioness.
He slipped his hand inside the metal bars
of her gate.

It was a very bad choice.

To the hungry lion, his arm looked like
dinner. Her instinct told her to catch her
meal, and she listened. She bit down on
the stranger's arm. He screamed and
screamed.

Just then Jeffrey drove up with a truck
full of meat. He could tell right away
things were not right. The entry gate was
unlocked and open. Screams were coming

from the big cats' cages. Jeffrey jumped out of his truck and ran toward the sound.

Jeffrey saw the stranger. He ran past Nitro, toward the lion cage. Jeffrey grabbed the man and tried to pull him free. But he wasn't as strong as the lion, and she would not let go. He never hit the animals, but he didn't know what else to do. The man was in serious danger.

Jeffrey picked up a metal pipe and swung at the lioness. At last, she opened her jaws, and the frightened man fell back. Jeffrey rushed the stranger to the

Did You Know?

Every tiger has stripes, but not all stripes are alike. In fact, none of them are. No two tigers have exactly the same pattern.

hospital. As he drove, he called the police on his cell phone.

Nitro would have to wait a little longer for his dinner. His owner was under arrest. He had not protected the stranger from the dangerous big cats.

Until that night, Jeffrey Harsh had broken no laws. Almost half of the states in the U.S. have passed laws to make it illegal to own wild animals like Nitro. Thirteen other states have some rules that say who can keep them and who cannot. The rest of the states have almost no laws at all. There, almost anyone can buy a wild animal.

Kansas is one of the 13 states with some rules. But the rules are not strong enough, said Sheriff Rod Taylor, the officer who arrested Jeffrey. Owners do not even need to take a class to learn how to care for a wild animal. If people like Jeffrey Harsh follow a few rules, they can buy big cats and raise them. And terrible things can happen.

Jeffrey didn't see it that way. He didn't think his big cats would hurt anyone. He thought since his animals were raised in captivity, or in cages, they would not act like wild animals.

"They were born in captivity," he said on his website, "and bottle fed, so they think they are human. They are as gentle and sweet as a house cat." He was wrong.

The judge gave Jeffrey a choice. He

could pay fines and spend months in jail, or he could give the big cats to people who knew how to take care of them. Jeffrey decided to give his pets away. The lionesses were headed to the Detroit Zoo. But this zoo didn't need any tigers. No zoo did. So where would Nitro and Apache go?

Sheriff Taylor called animal rescue experts for help. They told him about Carolina Tiger Rescue in North Carolina. Would they agree to take Nitro and Apache? That was the big question.

WANT TO KNOW WHAT HAPPENS NEXT?
Be sure to check out *Tiger in Trouble!*
Available wherever books and ebooks are sold.

INDEX

MORE INFORMATION

To find more information about the animal species featured in this book, check out these books and websites:

Crocodilians Natural History & Conservation
crocodilian.com

The Crocodilian Advisory Group
www.cag.crocodylia.com

St. Augustine Alligator Farm Zoological Park
www.alligatorfarm.com

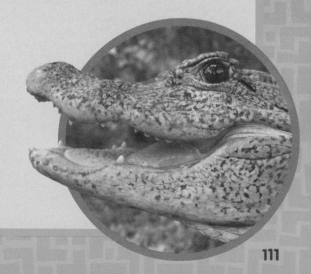

This book is dedicated to my mom, who always took me to the zoo when I was growing up. —Brady Barr

CREDITS

All photos courtesy of Brady Barr unless otherwise noted below:

Cover, Ann & Steve Toon/NPL/Minden Pictures; 20, Ivan Vdovin/Alamy; 22, Frans Lanting/Corbis; 25, Lori Epstein/National Geographic Stock; 34, Ralph Paprzycki/Alamy; 38, Anup Shah/naturepl.com; 41, AfriPics.com/Alamy; 46 (Background), Madlen/Shutterstock; 46, Rebecca Hale/NGS Staff; 81, Elisa Vagnini/age fotostock RM/Getty Images; 93, ichbintai/Shutterstock; 101, courtesy of Thomas County Sheriff's Office, Colby, Kansas; 102, courtesy of Carolina Tiger Rescue

ACKNOWLEDGMENTS

I would like to thank everyone who has ever helped me capture crocs. It is a long, long list of folks that spans 25 years of my croc field research and more than 5,000 captures. I would also like to thank my National Geographic Television field crews for not only filming my exploits but also helping to keep me safe over the years. Finally, I would like to thank all the crocs for letting me get close and learn more about them . . . and, most important, for not eating me!